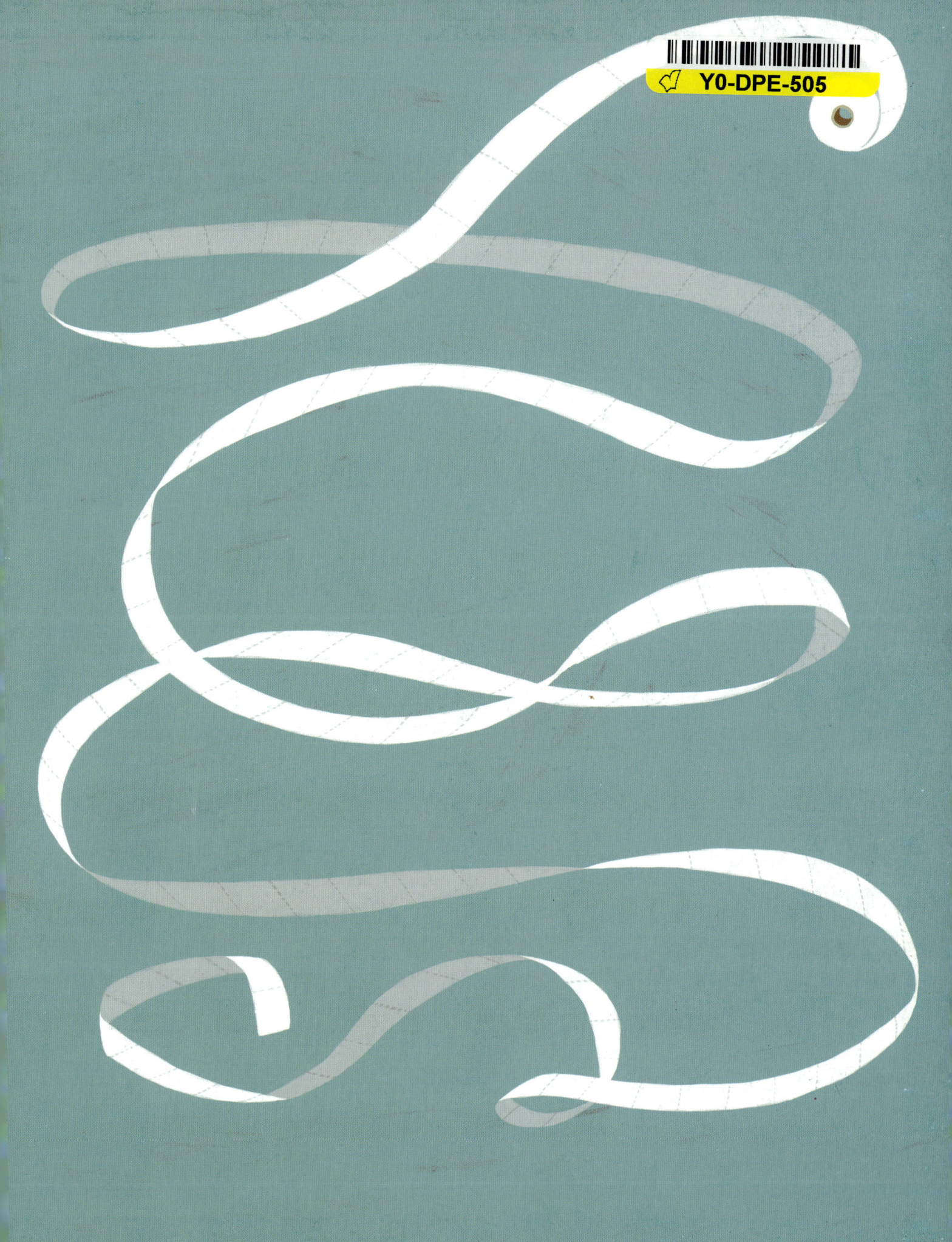

To a few of my favorite critters:
Aiden, Gable, Brody, and Ethan.
—H.V.

To little Ada.
—V.P.

Published in 2010 by Hallmark Books, a division of Hallmark Cards, Inc.,
under license from Sterling Publishing Co., Inc.
Visit us on the Web at www.Hallmark.com.

STERLING and the distinctive Sterling logo are registered trademarks of the Sterling Publishing Co., Inc.

Text © 2010 by Hope Vestergaard
Illustrations © 2010 by Valeria Petrone
The artwork for this book was rendered digitally.

BOK1159
Printed in China
JUL10

Hallmark ISBN 978-1-59530-313-4

Designed by Chrissy Kwasnik, who always washes her hands before leaving the bathroom

Potty Animals

What to Know When You've Gotta Go!

by Hope Vestergaard

illustrated by Valeria Petrone

STERLING
New York / London

Hallmark
GIFT BOOKS

Most critters are quite tidy:
a clean and pleasant lot.
But now and then you'll meet a few
young beasties who are not.

They don't mean to be messy.
They haven't got a clue.
Let's meet some potty animals
and tell them what to do.

Wilbur will not wash his hands—
a habit rather grim.
He doesn't think he picks up germs.
His hands look clean to him!
His parents ask,
    his teachers ask,
        the other kids ask, too.

And Wilbur always answers,
"I washed my hands, did you?"
His teachers ask if he used soap,
his hands do not smell right.
Eventually, he lathers up—
it's never worth the fight.

Wilbur, always wash with soap!

Wilma tends to wait too long.
She always keeps on playing.
She doesn't want to lose her turn,
or miss what kids are saying.

So Wilma hops from foot to foot.

She waits and waits and waits.

And when it's time, she has to race... but sometimes she's too late!

Wilma, don't wait!

Though **Arnold** has outstanding aim
to point and kick and throw,
he isn't always accurate
when it is time to go.

He hits the floor, he hits the lid, he hits the toilet seat.
Not much goes in the toilet bowl, which isn't very neat.

Yuck!
Lift the seat, Arnold!

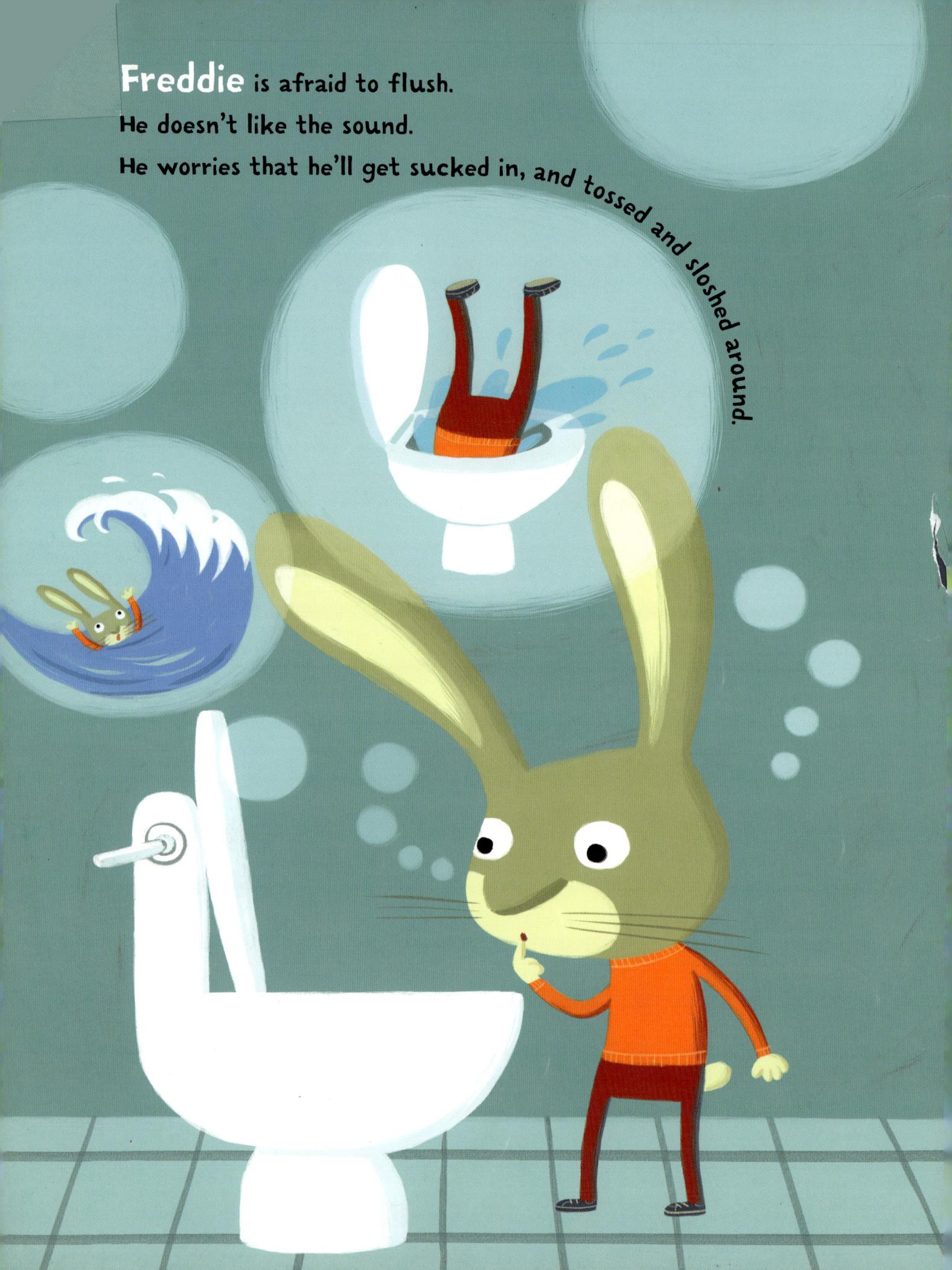

Freddie is afraid to flush.
He doesn't like the sound.
He worries that he'll get sucked in, and tossed and sloshed around.

So Freddie acts like he forgets.
He hopes that folks won't know
that he's the one who made the mess,
when it's their turn to go.

Don't forget to flush, Freddie!

Helga likes to lollygag,
she's never in a hurry.
But other kids who have to go
can really start to worry.

Sometimes she's having daydreams, sometimes she's reading books.

Sometimes she's at the mirror perfecting funny looks.

Hurry up, Helga!

Benji was a barger,
to everyone's chagrin.
He never knocked,
he didn't tap,
he marched straight in.
He had to pee
and didn't see
the critters waiting there.

One day Freddie barged in, too, and Benji got a scare.

Knock first, Benji!

When it's time to take a trip,
the teacher says to try,
but Roxanne never feels the urge
till cars go whizzing by.

Just when the bus gets up to speed,
she says she cannot wait.
It takes so long to stop and go,
she makes the whole class late.

Plan ahead, Roxanne!

Stanley had a secret trick
so he could stay outside.
When he was out and had to go,
Stanley liked to hide.
He'd find a tree and just go pee!

Sukey gets so thirsty,
she drinks and drinks and drinks.
Then something awful happens
when she catches forty winks.
She dreams of ponds and lakes and rain and floating down a stream,
and when she wakes from naptime...
she finds it's not a dream.

Go potty before you sleep, Sukey!

He wished that itch would go away,
but sadly, it did not.
The longer that he waited,
the worse the problem got.

Wipe every time, Georgie!

Agnes has a problem
with bubbles in her belly.
When they come out (and out they come!),
the room can get quite smelly.

Agnes just can't help it,
she has to let them out.
But after several episodes,
it makes her classmates shout:

Excuse yourself, Agnes!

Ziggy can be forgetful
when he is in a rush.
He doesn't forget to lift the seat,
and doesn't forget to flush.

He doesn't forget to wash his hands, and always turns out the light.
But when he comes out of the bathroom something's not quite right.

Check your zipper, Ziggy!

Feel free to use our restroom,
and please enjoy your stay!
We like to keep it spic-and-span—
we hope it stays this way.

If you forget your manners,
or don't know what to do,
think about the animals,
and what they'd say to **YOU**:

Plan ahead!
Don't wait too long!
Go potty before you sleep!
Excuse yourself! Knock first!
Be sure to lift up the seat!
Close the door!
Don't lollygag!
Never forget to wipe!
Wash your hands!
Flush and zip!
Always turn out the light!

If you and your little potty animals
have enjoyed this book,
Hallmark would love to hear from you!

Please send your comments to:
Hallmark Book Feedback
P.O. Box 419034
Mail Drop 215
Kansas City, MO 64141

Or e-mail us at:
booknotes@hallmark.com